Other work by Lance and Therèse:

Heart and Soul Meditations: A two CD
and cassette series by Lance Ware

Lot's Wife: A chapbook of poems
by Therèse Tappouni

Walking Your Walk: A Woman's Guide
to a Spirit Filled Life, a non-fiction
book by Therèse Tappouni

Note:

*All poems by Therèse are in this font, Lucida Calligraphy,
as is Ode To Marriage, which was written by both Lance and
Therèse.*
All poems by Lance are in this font, BernhardMod BT.

Second edition by Whole Heart Publishing
October 2001

Copyright ©2000 and Editing by Lance Douglas Ware
and Thérèse Amrhein Tappouni

Cover Photo: "Thérèse's Tulips" by Lance Ware
Cover Design: Thérèse Tappouni and Lance Ware
Printing by Hillsboro Printing, Tampa, Florida

Titles published or performed elsewhere:

"Song of Patience: Queen of Angels" performed on
Tampa's WMNF 88.5 FM, "Art in Your Ear" with
Joellen Schilke, 1998

Twenty poems from this work were performed at
Nuance Galleries in Tampa, Florida in 1998

"Original Scent" was published in *Pelican Tracks* in 1992

"Legacy" was published in *Lot's Wife* by Skin
Drum Press, 1994

"Letter From Here" was published in *Sunscripts*,
University of South Florida, 1999

Night Gardening

Passionate Poems
for the Beloved

Therèse Tappouni & Lance Ware

Lance Ware is a writer, teacher and Emotional Intelligence counselor in private practice. He wrote and produced *Heart and Soul Meditations*, a best selling series of CDs and cassettes to help people overcome creative and emotional blocks; to learn to relax, sleep and enjoy life. In addition, he teaches workshops alone and with his partner Therèse. They also present a unique performance of original poetry and music called *Sacred Space: Sensuous Souls*.

Therèse Tappouni is a novelist, poet, non-fiction writer and reviewer. She is also a mother, grandmother, community activist and president of Whole Heart. She leads workshops for women on the spiritual path, and performs with both Lance and the Undead Poets at various venues around the U.S.

*We dedicate this book
to you who join us
in celebrating a timeless
journey from fear to love.*

Poetry:
The secret religion
of the modern age.

Octavio Paz

Table of Contents

Section I: Tender Invitation

Section II: First Embrace

Section III: Drunk On Your Words

Section IV: Night Gardening

Section V: Love Letters

Section VI: Ecstasy on the Journey

Sacred Space

Thérèse and I are on a journey from fear to love. We are unalone. Most of us desire to be loved, to enjoy the thrill and passion of intimacy. Many other qualities can only be savored in the embrace of an evolving relationship.

When we're in love, countless aspects of life change rapidly. We are challenged to adapt and grow. Our sense of time shifts and our mood can be ecstatic. It's potentially as revolutionary as entering a mystical state of grace.

Yet we may not recognize the clues that reveal a soul mate, someone whose very breathing becomes a part of our own daily awareness of pleasure as well as confusion. A lack of experience with deep soul intimacy can lead to fears that separate us as quickly and mysteriously as love brings us together.

When we are blessed by love at first sight, timeless gifts are reborn in our hearts. These poems, written to and about each other and the passion of love, celebrate lifecycles of universal events. You may find the images are clues on your journey to discover a unique vision of ecstasy or grace that transforms sensuality and sexuality into a sublime synergy of physical and spiritual powers.

We offer thanks each day for the miracles that allowed us to meet and recognize in each other such startling, familiar characteristics as voice, eyes, ancient memories and a profound energy of love dancing through the phone. We began to remember and understand each other from our first words together. Now our goal is an intentional relationship that allows us to create and sustain a personal and professional environment we call *Sacred Space; Sensuous Souls*. Our chosen work enhances these close soul mate aspects of each other's writing, thinking and feelings.

Night Gardening was a free flowing delight to write and, we trust, will be a great pleasure for you to read aloud, to yourself as well as others you cherish. We are grateful for the rare opportunity to fulfill dreams of a lifetime. May this labor of love always be a blessing. Thanks for sharing so many experiences with us. We'd enjoy hearing from you.

Lance

Sensuous Souls

Love is an incredible tonic, one that sometimes leads us to leap beyond our usual abilities into the stratosphere, fearless and unaware of what we are attempting. And so it is with this book, a joyful project begun during the heat of a newly forged relationship.

Before we met in person, Lance and I were aware of each other as soul mates. As we explored our soul connection, new poems overflowed with a sensuality born of a powerful physical attraction.

When it appeared that we were fashioning a book, that someone other than my love would be reading my words, I contracted poetic amnesia. Everything I wrote lost focus as I attempted to control my creative urges for the possible desires of the marketplace. It wasn't until I realized the value of a book like ours that I moved from fear to astonishment and on to restored creativity. It was possible that the journey we were on could be a map for others like ourselves.

How was it that we knew of no writers living together in love who had written a book of poetry following the course of their passionate relationship? There certainly could be such a book, but whenever we asked those who should know, they searched their memories and mentioned the Brownings. Elizabeth and Robert wrote letters to each other, but these were collected by others. No one else has come to mind.

Lance and I discovered the therapeutic benefits of writing to one another early in our relationship, and knew that we could pass this on to others who would like to communicate in the fullness of their hearts and minds. We continue to be moved to write to each other about our deepest feelings because, no matter how much we talk, our poetry holds the truth of us.

Our greatest desire is that others will read what we have written and be led to share their love, longing, and fears with those they love. We have no doubt that we will continue to write to one another until, as I say in "Roses Are Enough," we "grow old together, moistening our mingled branches as long as the Universe says we are able." Thank you for inviting us into your life.

Therèse

Tender Invitation

What was sleeping above
your soul will rise
out of my mouth to heaven.

Pablo Neruda

Time of Love

We are meant to meet.
No doubt the mysteries
of birth and death thrive
in our dreams and desires.

Are we not here to speak
of love? A divine design
fills our expanse with time
and place, family and faith.

Children enter our universe;
greet us, grateful, as parents
rebuild the flesh and bone of
souls that need to be reborn.

We are meant to meet and
create a haven of feelings free
from the clock of technology
binding our hands with blame.

Begin by raising the heart
beat of a new community:
a language of universal souls,
rhythms of our own divinity.

Love courts the fabled union
foretold by spirit and friends:
mystics tempting these lands of
angels, carnal hearts and men.

Legacy

Deep in my center the knowing hums,
wordless, vibrating with meaning;
gift of my ancestors, hidden
in blood passed down through cords
of women. What she had, I want, knowing
it when the moon glints through the leaves
of the red oak, lays on my hands, lifts
the tiny hairs on my skin so when
the breeze skims scent off the salt flats,
it paints me as a Gauguin maiden.

I see one who leans against my back
like bark on a tree, curves round my spine
till it sings, strokes my hair. Sparks glint
from his fingers like butterfly wings.
I will know his voice, heard clear as chimes
from she who gave me the dream.
Patience wears thin at the hem when
the moon pulls waters of the tide
to mine and I am waiting on the dunes.

Together This Time

We arrive lonely, beyond
our points of no return.
How will you find me?

I've come to learn and love,
hoping your guides decide
to join with mine this time.

In the music of our hearts,
the soul's most eloquent voice
speaks to ease our fears,

helps us understand again
we are each other's home;
miracles on earth patrol,

somehow still alone until
we dream ourselves as one.
Give me clues to you tonight!

Meeting Again

Have we passed in the night
so close the air between us
rippled with held breath?

I have been patient, content
to tend and sort, plant bulbs
that won't show a leg until

April. Now I shiver with
expectation, know without
doubt you're just beyond

the bend of light that winter
brings, and I will not wait
for another spring.

You Do Exist

Many nights I awoke and
went to the roof to fly. I
spoke up to the universe,
searching for you again.

I know you exist. I hear
your language coming
through the garden of
my heart. Your words

glow nearby, growing
brighter in my ears. You
are calling me to blend
our colors and remember.

This much is blessed and
we are ready for more. I
feel you turn, walk to me,
the full moon in your hands.

Soul to Soul

Love is no longer a matter of where
and when but how soon can I fly to you,
how quickly will our souls collide, out here
where the stars are cold until we pass by

on our way to paradise. Breathing is
not necessary, though I recognize
your indrawn sigh as you catch up to me.
Love is no longer a matter of time

and space, but a tracing of longing and tears
as I come to you in long remembered
maps written on the skies in skirts of stars.
You, the caretaker of my heart, spinning.

Haiku for You

The world starts over
every time I feel your smile;
two dreams awaken

Ageless, true as trees
on a remarkable quest:
heaven's endless breath

Sunstruck, sky and sea
surrender differently
in this stellar wind

Sounds I did not hear
beyond shadows and spirit
dreamed us together

Your heart beats; I feel
this air, these colors are real;
you live within me

The world starts over
every moment we find love;
new dreams awaken

How Can I Keep From Singing?

Earth twirls,
a girl in a tattered skirt,
music of the spheres lifting her
as she watches herself
in the mirrored moon,
dancing at the ball.
Notes spray from her hem,
form a star-shaped staff
across the sky.
You and I
leap from octave
to octave,
crossing a brook
on worn stones,
fingers touching
each to each
like remembered dreams.
Together we compose our songs:
oceans of melodies
streams of harmony
and ponds,
still ponds of silent singing.

Divine Design

Only the open-hearted
are living in heaven today.
I've felt our fascination with
fear standing in our way.

There's a world of people
passing on the gifts they're
given first. Love's the pure
purpose each soul serves.

Life's a coming and going
of souls on rush hour trains.
Bless the exchange of another
day with no need for blame.

How many lyrics are written;
how many songs are sung
before we discover a true tone
where voice and vision are one?

Only the open-hearted
are living in heaven today.
I've felt our fear of soul
love standing in our way.

No one could ever take or
fill the places you hold love
so needed to assist and serve
cold souls in a lonely world.

Take the gifts you're born with,
find the purpose each one serves.
There's a life of trust and passion
waiting to be shared and learned.

How many hearts are searching;
how much love have we found
till we reach the level of wisdom
where lover and love are one?

First Embrace

I sleep but my heart wakes:
it is the voice of my beloved
that knocks, saying, open to me...

The Song of Solomon, Chapter 5, Verse 52

Night Secrets

It appears that everything is closed down,
night rules the shut-tight buds of the roses longing
for sun's shine. Nothing is really as it seems.

Deep in the garden's furrows, moonflowers raise
their heads, moist in the glow of the fullest time
of the month, just before the end of summer, before

last petals disappear under falling leaves. White
as narcissus, they flare on the vine, lift mouths
of desire toward the heavens until the sun's first

touch arches over the trees, stills their searching,
strokes them warm. Moonflowers sink once more
into themselves, wait until daylight turns to night.

First Embrace

I know I'm not alone.
I cannot be alone in this world
rich with romance dancing
beneath our silk suits of adventure.

On this earth of moist aromas,
arms and legs and new red lips
ripen in a flood of rose perfume
I picked and brought for you.

I know I've met men and women
living in love's waiting rooms.
We pray with hearts carefully keeping
passion and praise alive in open spaces
between the time of arrival and first embrace.

So many have shared my heart,
infinite families of old souls remain.
Dancers and healers, miracle births
and bodies long outgrown, lead beyond
everything seen or sensed or known.

We're drawn back to rendezvous
on this undivided planet more by dreams
of what two can do as twin flames than by
any drama of fortune, passion or fame.

I'm ready to share love's fire
of sun and moon with you.
Divine light dances closer and slower,
gathering sweet steps of final meditation.
Silent preparations focus one
energy flowing from my heart.

Intuition leads me through a nearly open door
to greet a distant pulse deeper than any desire.
I await the moment you enter and feel
our astral flares illuminate and heal
a long dark night of the soul.

In that pure moment we are
hungry to be unalone and alive.
In grateful relief we meet again,
after praying and listening at
so many locks with so few keys.

We finally discover a mirror of joy
glowing unclaimed behind
the northern lights of our eyes.

Finding a path so familiar
between the heart and soul,
we welcome each other
home in our arms,
warm and safe and whole.

Learning Your Language

Four years of Latin proved
no help at all until I
immersed my gaze in your eyes.
You called forth responses
in a dialect I'd forgotten.
No verbal cues birthed our
liturgy, the song of
two swans calling from
opposite sides of a fog
shrouded lake. I know you.
We talked where there was no need
for language; in dreams and wishes,
intention being everything.
The future came up behind
us and all we had to do
was listen. My understanding
splits open, ripe melon, all
seeds and juice. It was that easy.

Song of Patience

More and more I hear your voice and know
you understand. All the way, with open hands
that comfort, you guide me home to a land

within the sound of laughter. Colors of my heart
are clear. Distance is the fear we left behind.
Know why you have come and are divine.

There's a path before us, reappearing in the mist.
We leave the old outgrown noise, turn inside and find
our bliss in the pure, wet taste of love along the shore.

I feel stages of relief and hear washing waves
of peace heal our ancient, angry hearts.
Only God can come here for us;

only trust can unlock doors we've seen
but rarely opened in belief before.
Patience is the queen of virtue; understanding

comes our way. Old begotten fears can vanish:
drop like leaves beneath the light of one more day.
With you I feel the truth before the story's done:

from the window of the soul, through the eyes, beyond
control. We are free among old souls who have united,
one by one. Moving together, our journey has begun.

Patience is the queen of virtue; understanding
rules our house. Open feelings flow together.
Come inside me, let your arms and hair and mouth

release the past; be alive to love's new ways.
Beloved, you are my light at dawn. Patience
is the queen of angels; understanding is her song.

I Can't Remember

I can't remember when you
were not in my life, not
a part of my daily breathing,
my cellular structure, the sound
of wind in my bones. It seemed to
happen so fast, but we know there
was eternity in the composing,

virtuosos who refused to appear
until tonight, when we felt them
beside our bed waving goodbye.
You are seeded through me, newly
remembered melodies and lyrics
I never knew I knew. The shape
of you melds into the curve of me,

smooth as sculpture coaxed from
one piece of marble. I am mother
and mothered in one and the same
place, marveling at the miracle
of us as we flow through spaces
created by our presence. Hold my
hand, beloved, and I will sing

you vistas beyond the beyond
where the moon hides her other
side. She reveals herself to those
who love with the cool heat of eons
spent searching for the only mate,
freely chosen when the earth
was still a liquid child.

Made Flesh

From the valley looking east,
a line of trees bursts into applause
at the first morning breeze.

Ears of clouds pitch
forward to join the
harmony of blackbirds.

In a nearly empty memory,
sleep escapes a crowded
envelope of early light.

There is no time between
the distance and the dawn
browsing at our lips of love.

I couldn't stop,
I tried to sleep; there
were words to greet me

On the other side of
the sheets where I knew
you were waiting.

Unexpected Delights

I see the curve of his
back as he bends
to his task
and my breath
circles the known
universe.
It's not that I
don't see him
every day;
I do, but sometimes
I see him
without meaning
to and, oh my,
nothing prepares me
for the sight,
love streaming over
me like a warm
bath on a
chilly night.

Loving You

Till the harbour climbs on
the shoulders of this shore,

I will sleep in a haven of
memory and love, a circling

warmth of all you do, and
pray to be blessed with more

Ode to Marriage

You'll make such
a good husband

All the things we do
no one else has ever done

You'll make such
a good wife

All the love we feel
no one else has ever felt

We promise to cherish
through joy and through strife

You'll be such a good husband
You'll be such a good wife

Friends and Family say
as we start our new life

He'll make such a good husband
She'll make such a good wife

Your touch is so much
a part of my life

You make such a good husband
You make such a good wife

My dreams are our dreams
my life is now our life

You make such a good husband
You make such a good wife

Drunk on Your Words

Aphrodisiac without peer, words
fall from your mouth as pears from the tree...

Thèrése, from Drunk on Your Words

Fresh Kisses

My love's asleep
making fresh kisses;
some for me tonight,
more for breakfast.

So many I can taste
them before we touch;
our endless hunger,
unabated breath at lunch.

Kisses tossed at dinner:
plum tomatoes and olives,
Beaujolais and Brie;
bodies ripe with love.

In the distance, music from
a darkened room and bed:
we come from love's feast
more nourished than fed.

Awakening

You smell like bread baking, a slow warm scent that rises
to me with the sun, begins our day in an oven
of passion. The edges of my eyes receive

a benediction of light and I am filled with thanks
in a way that overflows with meaning. Outside the shell
of our love, the world begins the business of life, but we

are contained in the fragile protection of this tenderness.
I am no longer afraid. You hold me in the dawn,
mauve shadows painting your hands, my shoulders,

the sheets, until we are swimming in shimmering light
like rainbow trout. If I should slide over the edge of
dreaming, you would be there, your voice the gift of

movement in the sun's rising. Your fingers draw me
upward as I, and the Morning Glories, open
our mouths to drink the day.

Second Coming

My darling,
you're now
as quiet as
a breath
of peace,

meditation
breathing
dreams into
your sleeping
eyes and ears.

I follow you
home deep
into belief,
a rhythm
forever new;

we kiss and
you reply
with passion
and purpose:
our dream

opens me to
a journey's
meaning
I can read
and write;

for hours
you sleep
wrapped in
my erotic
thoughts

clearly
aware a
second
coming
is at hand.

Drunk on Your Words

Aphrodisiac without peer, words fall
from your mouth as pears from the tree

ripe and sweet, honeyed fruit to feed birds
glittering through the sun. We are free

to say truth in carafes of nectar, sure
that no one says love like you, and me.

Language is the only hope, the pure
version of who we are, what we'll be,

where we come from. What glorious star
makes love, for us, the heard, not seen?

We dream love in fragrances of myrrh
and oranges floating on an apple sea.

Cost of Creation

Tonight I bring you a mountain
of birds to our Carolina trees;

chimes in the sky sing
ancient words to me.

I cherish the singer,
my heart's dedication:

Your voice is worth
the cost of creation.

You're my goddess,
all rhythms and birth;

Your gardener of Eden
waters flowers of earth.

My Love Builds a Fire

Smoke is curling up over the copper lamp.
He adjusts the draft, adds pine, and flames
purify the air, painting the long bones of his
face bronze. I am back in time, this room

replaced by others somehow familiar,
other fires glowing in cabins and teepees,
rain tapping on the hickory. Contentment
rolls off me like the mist of this mountain

night in summer, and the heat of Florida
seems a dream lost in yet another memory.
Our world has stopped moving forward,
rotates instead, a wheel bound with love.

Morning, we lay late in the deep bed,
his hand curled in mine, a promise kept.
Our bodies warm to the banked heat that rests,
then leaps from the coals without warning.

Landscape

Bring me a skillful gardener
his tools in good repair;
When he goes down to my garden,
I will rise to greet him there.
                                        Therèse

My tongue overflows
the banks of contentment
to reach a river deep
within your skin.

Where else can a man
change the lay of the land
to find fountains that play
in the palm of his hand?

No wonder time goes by
so quickly here in heaven;
worlds are awakening wet
from your breath on my neck.

Breathing

You
come to me
on your breath,
sweet,
coated
with the scent
of strawberries.
Your body
warms the chair
across from me.
You talk
about what
we will do
tomorrow.
I am already
doing it,
feeling
your
hands on my
belly, knee
rising
against
my soul.

More than Love *(Therèse's Song)*

If I lose my hands
I'll still make love
unchanged in my
devotion to flying.

If I lose my way
I'll use lips and tongue
to open your kisses and
empty these clothes.

I'll revisit your garden
as moist as morning
to harvest a
second ecstasy.

I could be no one or
I could be known;
Nothing can stop the
love I've been shown.

I searched the world
to make sense of life;
all I made sense of is love.

You arouse my flesh
and miracles appear
between these hills by
the lake of pleasure.

We're coming to
navigate uncommon
lands, becoming
as carnal angels.

As we lose our fear
we'll feel more than
love reborn with our
memories of flying.

*We could be no one or
we could be known;
Nothing can change the
love we've been shown.*

*We searched the world
to make sense of life;
all we made sense of is love.*

Florida Night

Cassiopeia dips below the palms
this April night, honors our touch
with constancy, strokes the tear-tipped
petals of your lips with star-shine.

The Loon regains its voice as it rises
toward Summer, seems to lift on currents
of our joy. Moonflowers awaken,
drape perfumed vines over the dreaming

mangroves like Fred Astaire with Ginger
Rogers about to waltz on water.
We, too, dance on gentle waves, rise on
foam, then dip into the lull between,

bodies gone to Dolphin. Salt streaks your
thighs, sparkles like arrow points left on
the beach. There is no space between us:
we are wombed, arched in a primeval

dance drummed since time began. Can you hear
the voice of Great Egret chanting our love?
I leave my body, watch from heaven.

Night Gardening

From that very first look in your eyes,
I knew you and I were one heart.
Only our bodies were apart.
That was so easy, so easy.

"Miracles", Marty Balin, Jefferson Starship

After Reading Field Guide to Wildflowers

My pulse quickens, rising
to the brush of your mouth
inside my elbow; I want
another name for that place.

     Clitoria, her hooded
     irridescent blooms vine
     over dry soil without
     the aid of thorns or spurs.

Your breath blesses my temple,
warms my throat, raises
an ancient thrumming
from its humid burial.

     Artemisia, her rays of white
     or yellow named for the Goddess
     of love, prized by herbalists
     and medicine women. Sage.

Stieglitz said O'Keeffe painted
sex; let her speak for herself.
What I know is, when you touch
me, there, Black Iris unfurl

Belamcanda, Celestial Lily,
Fulva. In Iris, the broad sepals
often curve down, the three
narrower petals upward.

The cage of my shielding ribs
expands, becomes fertile ground
for your radiant bouquet.
My love, you smell of fresh earth.

The leaves are linear, folded
lengthwise astride the stem. Most,
but especially the long-petaled,
thrive in heavy wet soil.

There is no end to this lush
blooming, the wild profusion
of velvet petals and arched
stalks that is you and me.

Full Moon

Full moon Friday, something's new.
You call me and I touch you. We open
and enter a river of tender flesh. You
bathe me where the deepest currents
flow to reach these sacred shores.

Allow me to release the sweet perfume
of your thighs that know, despite the night,
I am coming to your country. As I enter,
you reveal a fertile path through fields
of hopes and fantasies.

I feel your garden growing moist within
my hands again. Rock and rest with me
upon a dancing land, here through all the
ages of our endless odyssey. We are eager
as breath, one skin whole and consummate.

Night Gardening

There is a stirring
going on
in a neglected glade.
Silently,
Night Blooming Jasmine
roots itself,
lays vines down,
runs them
along the ground
until heavy grasses
part,
reveal to the stars
a pomegranate,
seeds aglow like
burning rubies.
Quiet lies here,
thick as thoughts.
Drawn by heavy
scented blooms,
a man,
a questing mortal man
lays down amid Jasmine
to sleep.

The earth trembles
    you turn.
        Guided by the gods
            you lower your mouth
                to the succulent seeds.

Before dawn,
    in that sweet time
    of dark lifting,
        Nightingales come
            to sing in the bower

                that is now filled
                with fruit.

Coming Full Circle

Close to midnight again,
this bed is wide awake.
The dancers are aroused,
turning to perfection in a
season of perpetual emotion.

We were born here and have
come home so mating can begin.
Prehistoric waters flow between
us as we plunge ahead. Salmon
spawn near the mouth of our bed.

The colors around us are changing.
We taste the future of forgiveness;
know a place of primal wisdom.
Offspring become the end of us;
earth birth, new choice of the heart.

Hidden Veins of Gold

You gentled your mouth
on the vein
wound around
behind my knee
like the root
of a tree
and kissed it
with reverence,
named it worthy
of display.
I earned it in child-
bearing, think of it
as part of the hidden
river of life.
But when you
traced it with your
lips, I saw it:
beautiful, branching up
inside my thigh,
bringing rich blood
to the leaves
of me
blooming
in my secret places,
the roof of the world.

The Reign
of Fertilization

there's a history of our hearts,
how they open warm and strong
as each day dawns, wherever
new life begins and belongs.

your heart welcomes my
wet confessions of love,
squeezing blood for my
kisses to bloom above.

I come to grow here
in your garden I've
only seen when dreams
are waiting for meanings.

miracles begin to feed us, fresh
from a planet of breasts and lips,
as the reign of fertilization frees us
through time-ripened thighs and hips.

Eating

Meals used to be eaten
with an eye on the clock
and a worried calorie counter
in the head chiming in everytime
something tasted particularly
good, a signal taught in years
of classes on the dangers of food.

Then I met you. Now, meals
are sensual adventures in taste
meant to be savored over lengthy
periods of time. We eat to have
an excuse to sit side by side
feeling the flavor of skin, calf
to calf, the excitement of lips

wet with oil of the olive only
inches away. I never ate an
oyster before you placed one
in my mouth, an offering of
salt and life. Finger foods are
favored in this life of the senses,
feeding being as important as eating.

Your fingers in my mouth, a shift
in perspective that changes every
thing, even the taste of raw tuna
and ginger or a cinnamon stick
dipped in cappuccino. Wines were
only juice of the grape until you
poured a glass of champagne for

me and stirred it with a strawberry,
red as only winter berries can be
in this part of the world. My taste
buds are being trained to new heights,
and paté is almost more than I can bear
when you spread it on an apple. Who
could have told me what joy resided

in a cobalt blue plate scrolled
with darkest chocolate, home to
a Kahlua drenched slice of Tiramisu?

Original Scent

I am more, much more
than icing on your cake.
My harvest of flesh
lies within your memory
morning or night
as smooth hard caresses,
fork to fork, awaken you.
Hungry, we smile again.

My hands arrange an orchestra
of orchids for dinner;
my lips on your neck stir
the warmth in your breasts.
Eyes hold unknown words
between fingers and thighs
as graceful sounds of skin
fold around our loving meal.

You are more, much more
than modern history claims:
only you can change your name
planted in my tongue, deep
within our menu of intentions.
No others open and enter
the same taste of tender flesh
to mix untamed ingredients.

Ancient appetites are fed
but traces of longing lie
fresh and ripe as tastebuds
until the untimed thrust of hunger
comes again to bind us in
that sweet sweating blend--
the deep original scent
of a woman and man.

Patience

I have made my heart a wilderness, that the wildflowers
of Thy love might blossom there.
              Paramahansa Yogananda

I long only for the rain,
a water hyacinth thirsting
under a searing sun. You, my love,
my patient love, are honeysuckle,
come to gentle the weeds, make way

for the sweet violets. We lie by
the pond, where lily pads strong
enough to carry our dreams wait
to float on Spring's showers. A
wilderness becomes a bower,

a place as verdant as Eden as,
at last, the life-giving moisture
drifts through the trees, sparkles
on our skin like ice on spiderwebs,
touches our tongues with life.

River Rider

When I point my face,
these timeless lips, other
than at your known mouth,
I'm heading south, some
where deep inside your valley,
river of the earth's hips.

If I could curl my tongue
anywhere on this world,
I would taste your tide,
a river rider southbound
on memories' many trips
to these fragrant shores.

If I could kiss away again
the tears of hidden days,
to love you well tonight,
I would clear a space for
us within this garden on
the inner edge of evening.

If I could tune my heart
by any known rhythm or
the lights of our minds,
I would ask you now to
surround me with skin
to guide me in the dark.

Night Flying

t told me, but I didn't believe
t I could fly, lift right off the bed
wings of a sacred Raven, your
ds and mouth the instruments of flight.

ing you above, then below me,
t rose up my spine, warmed the air
pdrafts carried me just below our
ing. Next time, I know, I will leave

body, go straight as an arrow to
us and present my calling card;
ue-black feather dewed with
rs torn straight from disbelief.

Love Letters

The very touch of the letter was as if you had taken me all into your arms.

Anaïs Nin in a letter to Henry Miller, 6 August 1932

More than Birth

Be careful; I have burst
apart and have no name
for what remains of me.

A world unknown is
growing through skin;
my nails have changed.

This is more like birth
than spring renewing;
my heart is part of you.

Through us, a new planet
is passing giant bodies
of water and blood.

Worlds live within words;
I know how they arrived
here and what they need.

They're closer than flesh;
more intense than any love
I have known or heard of.

With you, my heart grows
wider than life or death; no
memory was ever this size.

I have more than fear
as you move in my life,
coloring me with meaning.

I do not recognize
who I am today;
Stay with me.

I have become too large
to ever live alone; to
ever return to myself.

Taking A Chance

Sometimes, when I said I needed you,
I whispered it for fear
you would run from
the room, take shelter in old
ways of being alone.
A cold child huddled
inside me, asked to be held
and raised into the light. Now,
you hear me and gather me in.

You bid me good morning, light
kiss on the nape of my neck
familiar as bird song
or the rose-glow of dawn
streaking our bedroom window.
Your voice lifts me from sleep, slow
and gentle, shows me to this day
with love so fresh I am
baptised in surprise.

Lips of Heaven

like silence rising
from lips of heaven

I try to tell you but
I may be too late

to stop this moment
of indescribable love

from disappearing into
my imperfect memory

where even the pain of
lost love lies forgotten

like silence rising
from lips of heaven

Trusting

Trusting is opening your heart
to hear the sounds of another
heart beating in fear of opening.

Opening is trusting your heart
to bear the pain of another's
heart scarred by careless wounds.

Wounding is closing your heart
to cries of longing from another's
heart that aches to open to love.

Loving is taking what that heart
gives and holding it, another's
heart, to your own like a new life.

Life is trust, surrounding the heart
joining the beat of another's
heart and another and another

and another.

Night Lights

Our bed backs up
to the closet
as I pull in
to your thighs.

Night lights open
the drapes by hand,
each one drawing in
dark as they pass.

I shut my eyes
close my ears
to the sudden
hiss of fear.

Light fights to be
heard in a roomful of
words that bruise and
tear every dream.

Outside, the race
of tires patrols
our wet night
streets of desire.

As natural fears relax
acquired ones come true;
I turn into you,
sleep in the haven of

Memory and love
in the arms of
all that you do,
alive where sirens

Of sorrow have failed
to follow the passing
of those we love;
We are hard of hearing.

A Question of Believing

Chill wind whispers
on the hearth
but I will not
be denied,
though curtains blow
and pillows toss
in cool cotton
discomfort.

Under my heart
in a place
used for storage
words of need
seeds of longing
escape into
a space reserved
for love and

take their chances.
I could catch
my death of cold
or you might
dance right into
my words
and hold me close.
Anything,

anything
is possible.

Solar Eclipse

The sun burns our memories
coined by lips planting love;
a daily tempest before
separation. Racing away,
a universe is your absence.

Eclipsing even the ecstasy
of yesterday's feast, paper
flies from my hands. A
landscape of ink and desire
darkens solitude with ritual.

I sacrifice 99 unused kisses;
only yours can never be rejected
by my blood. I work all night,
fresh words between fingers,
your gravity pulling me home.

Letter From Here

Night blankets Grandfather mountain,
pulling veils of mist up the bony
cliffs like a shy girl dressing for bed;
a reflection in the window
my only companion. In that same
glass, fire on the hearth flares across
Cassiopeia riding higher
as earth pulls herself down into

winter. Alone is hearing the song
of wind in ancient Sourwood trees.
Alone is sketching your face behind
closed eyes, tracing over memory
of the long arch of your foot against
mine beneath the cold sheet. Alone
is talking inside myself, writing
words down, wanting you to answer.

Creation

No one hears the final
words of ancient verses
sung before the fires.

Next to nothing remains
to be seen above the
windowsill of childhood.

Say you have just climbed
upon the cross of stars
to sit beside our moon.

You know these are not
the last great hollow
promises of tomorrow.

I couldn't stop, I
tried to sleep; there
were words to greet me

On the other side of the
sheets where I knew
you had been waiting.

Open, open again your
arms and eyes; I know
only emptiness fulfilled.

Beyond the inner lining
of remorse and tears,
a soft voice echoes:

Come now, patch
my holy fingers
with the flesh of kisses.

Forgiveness is the chamber
next to my own heart;
I'll meet you here tonight.

Sliding Through

space as though there were no energy patterns
    waving back and forth like amoeba, no web
of connections from that butterfly in Africa
    to the coast of Florida. From my bed
to yours, a mere thousand miles traveled
    in milliseconds, the proverbial blink of my
eye sees me sliding under your covers,
    curving round your shoulder, fleshless
shawl of sleep and love greeting you quiet as
    snow. In the morning I wake to the ghost
of you dusted on my skin, born new in the smell
    of shared dreams sprinkled in my hair.
In the afternoon you phone and tell me
    about your sleep, how unusually deep for you
in your childhood room far away. I tell you how
    I arrived and feel your smile traveling
at the speed of butterflies across the continent,
    know it will come just as I go to sleep here,
in the sacred space you will share before too long,
    though it is already way too long.

Full Moon Again

Erotic phantom, as you travel,
may the secret voice of Spirit

guide your every breath; that you
return with time to widen the lunar

harbor of my heart beside the bay.
Share the light within you; let it raise

a floodtide of intentions. Reveal your
inner peace, stronger than mother's blood.

Daily meditations bring a newly noticed
presence to our circles of devotion. I am

grateful; You have graced my heart with
gardens in the wilderness of your love.

Missing Parts

I am missing the taste of sea salt
where your neck becomes shoulder,
the small pulse that shows itself
in the barely visible depression
below your throat, fragile as the web
in a new born baby's head.

When you're not here, I listen
for a voice during breakfast,
decide grapefruit juice is all
I can swallow in this silence.
I turn on the radio more often,
dial in classical, moody stuff;

watch Jeopardy, argue with Alex
Trebek. Work becomes a mission.
I keep the bathroom so shiny
it appears unused. Black loafers,
saved for dancing, look forlorn
in the corner. The bed stays half-

made as I fold the spread to the
side and leave your pillow under it,
telling phantom burglars that you
are home, in bed, with me. I curl
around my pillow but my back gets
cold where you usually curve

around me. I wear nightgowns.
I see friends, movies you won't like
and eat fast food. When you come
home, my shoulders will soften,
the TV will get lonely and the bed
will come to life. The parts will flow

together again, filings to a
magnet, blood to our heart.

Ecstasy on the Journey

*Angel, look away. / I cannot afford to yield the las
defense,/ To go back/ "Not back, but deeper"/
said the angel, folding his wings/ To wait.*

May Sarton from The Fear of Angels

Mundane Angels

There are parts of my life that
don't know what love fears

like hours of my day
that run out of light.

I'm losing my fear for
a new type of vision;

there are things we can't say
to make sense of tonight.

I've learned without you
there are no mundane angels

and no words for now
as good as love feels.

Dream at Five A.M.

Your voice lifts like smoke,
drifts round my legs, curls
into my ears, whispered messages

caught by cupping my palms
into nautilus shells.

Your words, sonorous as temple
gongs, tangle between my fingers,
hang in my hair as beads of dew.

I go down into their company
and sleep.

Heart and Soul

Across this planet of wars, worries
and deals shines a light so clear, a
touching and healing of souls so strong,
I awaken and travel to you,
to renew our first embrace.

We know we don't want to
come home and be owned.
I'd rather be held in the light where
love is growing gifts of the soul.
I feel you relax, and know my heart.

There's so much to share as we go.

Why Are We Here?

We are a forest
hands
grasping, telling,
begging
taking the land,
selling,
giving no thing
in return.
How can we see the sky?

Some will make
joy-filled
sound, spread
palms
down, receive
sanctuary,
turn cacophony
into rhythms
made in the earth.

I feel it
through
my feet.
I can't stand still.

Bear Fruit

Go deep into the knot of loneliness
before the closing door of love
beneath the blue geography
of the regular army sailing
the streets of fear abandoned.

Journey to the hall of time; no one
enters without the gift of grace.
Leave no empty messages for
those who follow: for I have
followed and found you.

Announce yourself and mount
the steps to work a key
into the frozen lock of fear.
Reveal the knocking of my heart
throughout these ages longing

to be honored as a mate.
I love you and have done
for a very long time.
Forget not once that I come
for more than your touch.

I cannot be removed.
Wonder is the present edge
of flesh upon my tongue.
You have encountered me
up close and now I turn

to jump into your smile,
feeling your breathing, hearing
the beating rhythm of love,
leaving sleep untouched and
morning already unmade.

Persuasive eyes of passion lie
between us and the future.
Bear fruit upon this tree
of mine inside your garden.
I cannot be content with less.

Morning Gardening

Awakening with the sun is not
our normal way, but when you rise
to the melodies of birds, I follow.
Early, day is cool, moist, and wide

awake; the gardener is the same.
The garden is sleepy and seductive
accepting the tending of hands and
mouth with growing interest.

Making love as the mists float below
our window, we are not drawn
elsewhere to empty the day from
aching heads or to adjust bodies

heavy with dinner. We are new
as morning dew, sleepy-eyed yet eager
as if we were thirty again, the maples
still saplings. We promise each other

more long, liquid, silver mornings,
and curl back to front, content to be
adrift in the heavy perfume of after-love.

Between the Stars

Born blessed, we found each other long ago.
Happy Anniversary!! Pleasures of the flesh
still fresh in my mind, my garden is aroused.
My goddess, sky clad in the evening glade,

We have everything carnal angels adore.
Love lets souls pass through our pores,
beyond physical mating as mystics arrive
through the colored air of morning.

Tonight, the western sky is alive
with people flying home, high
overhead where birds live fast
and flee the passing of us all.

Between the stars, clouds of souls
land in the flesh of families known
by the long slow march of men and
women shopping for perfect babies.

You do not know and shall not own
the road they walk alone; a sure-footed
clock of hands and feet, blood and bone
trades their time for each moment of love.

At dawn, this eastern sky is fire above
the filter of another circling sea. Be ready.
Life is coming to a head, returning from a
world beyond the liquid center of our bed.

The Face of My Beloved

What I see there is not visible
to others
shared visions
lived together in other
dimensions
other times
stranger places.
Even when my eyes are
closed
there is a whole being
as long as part of him
touches me
skin to skin.
Science explains
but I don't understand
the way a part
becomes
a complete thing.

There is a way our faces
fit, though that doesn't
explain
bone to bone
slope to rise
hollow to hollow.
When he is
away
there is a vacancy
in my energy
an absence
of life
in my
life.

Hear the Distance

How can you hear the distance so clearly?
We've been many places remembering
why we return to this beautiful earth.
Together, we survive the difficult times.
With passion and care, you touch me again.

Trust releases the past to unite us.
I am open to salvation;
You remind me why and how.
The better I know my heart and soul,
the more I learn to give and grow.

I offer you comfort when change is near:
to broaden our vision, to go beyond hope,
to sing something special, to ripen in wisdom.
There's worlds to be found in
the closeness surrounding our souls.

Never Again

For Lance, on our anniversary with all my love.
August 7, 2000

Not again in this lifetime, the glorious gold net
of amazing Grace that fell upon us when we met,
the crescendo of horns that arose from our deepest
places of knowing, escaped our mouths in notes
so sweet, even we were spellbound. Colors blazed

through tropical gardens that had never known
such orange existed, the color of sunset in winter
draping the trees like Spanish moss. Mysterious
birds nested outside the windows of our house,

their song wooing mates in a hypnotic spell of warble
and trill that swelled as dawn broke and scattered
drops of gold among the hibiscus. We walked above
the beach, sand soft as talcum sifting below our feet,

the ocean murmuring bedtime stories of lives lived
in Spain and Brazil, promises made and kept. We
will not speak of future blessings, my love, for we
are content to lie here in the rosy arms of today.

Seed to Soil

The wait of wisdom holds us
here as tides of learning pass
through our lips to find familiar
pleasure in surrounding lands.

Over that hill, pastures welcome
ancestral harbors at our shores.
We are closer than houses now,
fenced with children on the go.

Reunions enrich the fallowed
homestead, memories of ages
made from flowers and earth.
Land of abandoned love restored.

This night I enter, breathing slow.
Over different roads our families
come to meet at pre-determined
doors. We hope to reach them.

Here, one light reveals us all. We
move on till we transfer our fire
from flesh to earth, seed to soil;
can rest our beauty and turmoil.

We are gardeners with decisions today:
to tend our families and friends with
love and forgiveness that set us free.
There are no richer moments than these.

Roses are Enough

You bring me roses for no good reason except that you love
to bring me roses. I watch them bloom, smell their perfume
in the bedroom and strip their blossoms for potpourri before
they die. Somehow, it is important that I don't see them die.

I bring you flowers that wet the sheets, live forever,
anoint you with the scent of love. We are in love with
flowers, bouquets of wild herbs, sage and sweet grass
for the altar. We are in love with limbs and skin, leaves

that flutter in salt drenched breezes warm from summer.
Rooted, we will grow old together, moistening our mingled
branches as long as the Universe says we are able. When
one of us dies, the other will feel soft rain on the skin,

lie down on the wet ground, and watch tulips birth
their fragile tips through the soil. They will look
amazingly like us in the glory of our middle years
when we showered each other with flowers.

If you wish to order a bunch of our books, please send
$14.95
h plus tax for the original version or $24.95 each plus tax
for the full-color, signed, limited edition.

Remit check or money order to:

Whole Heart
P.O. Box 1011
Indian Rocks Beach, FL 33785-1011

You may also order books and CDs from our web sites:

Lance Ware: www.livingpeace.net
Thérèse Tappouni: www.wholeheart.net

If you would like to contact us or find out
about workshops, please check our websites.

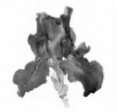